GW01607873

THE BRIGHT INVISIBLE

WILLIAM J. PHILBIN

THE BRIGHT INVISIBLE

VERITAS PUBLICATIONS

First published 1983 by
Veritas Publications,
7-8 Lower Abbey Street,
Dublin 1.

Typography and cover design by Liam Miller.
Typesetting by Printset and Design Ltd.
Printed in the Republic of Ireland by Genprint Ltd.

ISBN 0 86217 116 4

The author gratefully acknowledges his indebtedness to Father John McMackin whose counsel has been of invaluable assistance to him in shaping these pieces.

Some of the pieces in this volume have appeared in the following publications: Horace to Virgil, *Latin Poetry in Verse Translation,* Riverside Press, Boston; *Es Sacerdos,* Vexilla Regis, Poor Clare Christmas, *The Tablet;* The Pope in Ireland, *Sunday Independent;* On Remembering Neil Kevin, Saint Oliver Plunkett, *Irish Independent.*

CONTENTS

No player will every audience engage
Identically, no chef for all palates cook.
Mind favours are particular and a book,
Collecting people, head-hunts each's page.

Pace Ausonii

THE BRIGHT INVISIBLE

There is no writing of mine on this subject nor will there ever be; for it cannot be put into words like other objects of knowledge. . . . You live together in the pursuit of this thing; and then suddenly, like a flame kindled from a leaping fire, it comes into your soul and feeds itself.

Plato

Eia nunc ergo, Domine Deus, doce cor meum ubi et quomodo te quaerat, ubi et quomodo te inveniat. . . Ad te videndum factus sum, et nondom feci propter quod factus sum.

Saint Anselm

Quis infinitum Deum. . . scire gloriabitur? Quem nemo vidit unquam ut est. Nullus itaque praesumat quaerere investigabilia Dei, quid fuit, quomodo fuit, qui fuit.

Saint Columban

1

We who exert to peer
Beyond percipience
Who hijack thinking's gear
Out of experience;

Uncramped by cosmic bounds
To be prevented still
By opaqueness that impounds
The Bright Invisible;

Spry to pursue, to share
Rocketing minds' transgress
(Fool-erranded too by their
Eriugenal excess):

Is our aggrandisement dross
From reconnaissance withstood?
Is it prescribed to cross
Thought's edges to think God?

Is ampler recompense
For homage decoyed in
The arabesques of sense
Than search where these begin?

2

Knowing is livelihood
To mind, as eye needs see;
Mind whose importunate food
Is Who could not but Be —

Stable, uttermost source
Of haphazard; alive
Of quintessential force;
Nothing's correlative —

Source which on homing sense,
Time-space riven abroad,
Twitches us whence
We origin, God toward.

3

Deep as enquiry delves
What have we understood?
Uncomprehending ourselves
Shall we adumbrate God?

Plato reasoned the soul
Body-free, God-sped by
Purgings; but God goal
Disavowed to espy.

Artefact figuring Him
Sinaic interdict drew;
If mind lens could limn
Might not hand craft hint true?

Moses parleyed with God,
Bid never so near,
But showed, for fire and cloud,
More listener than seer.

If He was One apart
To Isaiah shall we adhere —
One whom the wise of heart,
With Job, unsee and fear?

All we indite of God —
Augustine's plea — is lest
We are attaint of fraud,
Prophesying the unprofessed.

Better do than know
Goodness, Austin said;
Is our rubric below
To go darkly led.

4

Yet Hippo would pierce the veil.
Purposed love he held given:
Should only notioning fail?
May intents not contend even?

Learning's sum is less
Than love, Aquinas knew:
But his cup for blessedness
Tilted toward the true.

Arid, austere our task?
But they who love by law,
With no question to ask,
Is their stint without flaw?

Absit filigree care
Be out of focus above.
If labour doubles for prayer
Why not thinking for love?

And when attachment is weak
And mortgaged here and there
May curiousness not speak
Reflexes of prayer?

Nothing aspirants do
Heavenward meets lidded eyes;
Faith effervesces through
Wonder and surmise.

Allowed none shall unravel
All of God is to know,
Is it not due we travel
Where His visa will go?

Elect spirits fare
By avenues that transcend,
But should supremes of prayer
Intellect obeisance end?

Shall excellent grudge space
To good? Might diversity
Of virtue's broad embrace
Foil high insistency?

5

Thought fuels no beam that can
Monitor You but our
Rummage is richer than
Apprehension's power.

Dialectic, debate
Leave us no less apart:
But stamp mind's meagre estate
And discipline high heart

Toward deferring to love
In precedence to declare
One dizzyingly above
Our homespun good true fair.

6

If we have Adamed Your
Otherness but masking name,
Earth-modelling cynosure,
Does shortfall mandate blame?

If neighbour knowledge is gained
As infant sprawls and creeps
Are summits attained
After no fumbled steps?

We have dimension alone
To frame Infinity;
Fancy but mirrors our own
Blow-up identity.

Earth is all evidences
Of ways the All-author went
But where have presences
Left windowing dent?

Our eyes are filled with seeing
The stir and change of things;
Where are thought-moulds for Being
Naked of happenings?

From what metaphysical tower
Are gossamer bearings sought
On unpositioned Power
Summoning worlds from thought?

Yet God — not such as we —
Unsighted can enfold
With nearer intimacy
Than lovers that behold.

7

Can One who interveins
Universality
Transcend while He sustains?
We inhabit mystery.

Will concept condense Un-
containable in speck space?
Unending Unbegun
Abridge to eye-blink embrace?

Can Still be least inert —
Of intellect, will compact,
Effortlessly alert
In all-attaining act?

May Singleness align
With particulars unblent
Of Compeer Triad Divine
Essentially unrent?

Is knowing of such weight,
Loving such merit
As Son will generate
And will send Spirit?

Does equalness consist
With inter-origins? Do
Mind metrics subsist
Where limitless is true?

Scriptures deliver no
Clairvoyance of God;
Philosophies vertigo
Chasing infinitude.

8

Your praise Perfection excelling
Behind curtains of seeing
Is animate in the telling
Of the Word within Your Being —

O Living Love emerging
Of Fatherhood Filialness
Coincident Unconverging
In intercircling caress —

Godhead akin with us
Twice begotten Son
Your crossing and cross
Man's Godhood has won

Matrix and Pulse of living
Whose Spiritkind we share
Giving and forgiving
Contain us in Your care.

9

In Me you see the Father
And in My doing you know:
Is not here to look rather
Than pry where no lights show?

Jesus is Good translated
To actual from abstract;
God-counterpart, created
Creation's end to enact.

But God in flesh was shrouded —
Emptied, Paul said — save for
When stooping Heaven unclouded
Seeing for three on Tabor.

We are dim unperceivers —
Millennia between —
Albeit especial believers,
Our charisma not to have seen.

Godhead in Christ is featured
For faith, not to descry;
And flings, curtailed, encreatured,
Gauntlet of How and Why —

When Heaven's assuredness
Intermits to remedy
Man's fault by God's distress
Comes mateless mystery —

Divine liaison hour
With anguish could we compel,
Key-holder of hearts and our
Father, we who rebel?

Christ is credential that clinches
God being love, and yet
Are we nearer by inches
To faith with manifest met?

No clues the Schools afford
God concept enable:
We harvest metaphor
Symbol analogue label.

God-seen-in-what-is-made
Paul preached but in work-out
We may feel we have strayed
Into knowing what God is not.

10

We cupboard every crumb
Of mind manna and weigh
But not compute their sum
Nor construe what stretched words say.

No panel of the firmament
Thought-infiltrated will
Unshutter minute splint
To point the Ineffable.

God is late heard: *Forgoing*
Phantasm brings countervailing
Knowledge by unknowing
And fulfils by failing.

God not by doorbell known
Nor spoil of contraband
Your enterprise alone
Brings us to understand.

Peremptories to know
Dissolve in unrest to see
Your oncome overthrow
Himalayas of mystery

With uncreated light
Which in a flash redeems
The long catch-nothing night
The miscarriage of dreams.

NAZARETH

The world's deliverance hinged to a girl's consent
One Nazareth moment when Archangel spoke
For God and Mary for all human folk,
Her *fiat* enabling the divine intent.
She was the doorway when the Almighty bent
To becoming man and from her body unbroke
All that incorporates one of our kind He took.
Not handmaid Mary, not mute instrument:

She, at the fulcrum hour of history
When God should incarnate so Christ might give
God-loded atonement come yet of Son of Man,
Sole confidante of the Salvation plan,
Demurred, endorsed — God's mate in the mystery
Of His manmaking in Whose life we live.

BETHLEHEM

Foreseeing was not to the fore, if one may dare say,
When the Bethlehem journey was set up. Were all not aware
From Jerusalem occasions late comers are apt to ill-fare?
Could not word have been carried by party less prone to delay?
And must Mary really have roaded it? Was there no way
What was plain might be pleaded, her husband and kinsman being there
For her answering? They were date-sure: who ever had mark to compare
for invoice of birth with her unforgot angel-came day?

But again if a girl is embodying God may she dare
Have qualms of His childing? Can His scheme on our scheming depend?
If we trip shall not He supersede us and more than amend?
Grace roots in ineptitude. Was the whole Gold-embroiling affair
Not perquisite of poverty, of our needing Him by us to repair
Our bungle and botch of life's wayfaring, Adams to the end?

ETIAM PRO NOBIS

He savoured the world He was Word of, God-made, good:
The swirl of skies and seasons, sun wind rain
Contending in collusion. Tares might remain
But not void fig-tree — much is due from wood.
The comity of sheep and shepherd stood
For His Realm's emblem. He watched lilies gain
Showing beyond Solomon. Sparrow's fall, sea-lane
Shoal-cluttered He heeded Who fed the multitude.

His being about blessed earth business and He knew
All of our doing — thieves' stratagems, stewards' treasons;
How from within us seeds every malfeasance.
Yet we it was He was drawn to — I and you,
And not in judgment not for revenue
But to agonise unassuageable love's appeasance.

CALVARY

Spring was not special that year in Galilee but there ran
A ripple above waterlines, a distraction of currents. *He is come,*
The Man of Isaiah, we have stood where He houses. The hum
Of His rumour would street-spill villages as Isaiah began
To enact, would thoroughfare wilderness as beyond-plan
Courtesy at Cana became quickening of crippled and numb
To sentience, to pardoning grace that was principal: Heaven's sum
Of fecund resource in labour for Heaven-birth of man.

What morning how darkened! Spring's way into summer how slow!
Kingdoming was torted to trespass. One Who only is good
Was thugs' plaything, Barabbas outbid. How far from what should
Be such sickle's swathing, wooing's welcome! Yet how should men know,
Calvary unclimbed, what glints from no favour-flow,
The whelm of love that availed the death of God?

ANOTHER ENVY

He was no connoisseur of our courtesies:
Reject arrival, bundled in random manger,
Peddling the unprized, betrayal's footbather, a stranger
On our rote roads, eccentric to categories.
He assailed assurances with contraries,
Addict of deprival, beyond dissuasion exchanger
Of proffered power for dear pursuit of danger:
One seeming not to discern the things to His peace.

His lights are sightings by whose side wine sours,
Suns darken; His coveting is not our pleasure;
To grant not grasp brims His fulfilment measure.
His word is of another envy than ours,
Of unentanglement with things that empowers
Limbering of limbs for Heaven's Kingdom's seizure.

WORDS

Words are our liveliest making Roger Bacon said:
Midwives and moulds of thought, spirit parturition,
Coin of mind commerce, self-knowledge's condition.
In words idea is winged, percipience wed
With residuary wisdom of the dead.
Words hunger for deeds, sparkle with intuition
Of time's better devisal; language has mission
To conjure unfallen worlds, *poiesis* bred.

Voices have vogue, expire. Once have been spoken
Pivotal words, signals delineating
World of the Word, healing, redintegrating
Mankind with God: *Come, sin-sunk, sick, life-broken,*
To Life and have for metamorphosis token
Words body of God from earth fruits incarnating.

PANTOCRATOR

There was an absolute about Him for master
Of man and circumstance. Beyond Abraham
And kindling stars outstands His sheer *I am.*
He jostled nature's rhythms in token of vaster
Arbitrament of blessedness and disaster.
Seeing Me you see the Father; deviced in a lamb
I am death's countermand, life-endowing; clam,
Graft, batten on me. No mould He of our plaster —

More universe keystone. His wrist flick wields world sway.
But miracle but manipulates: He would divide
The Infinite from felicity; eclipse, elide
The divine difference; diminish Godhead to prey
Malignity might devour on a stark day
When God was most divine, being crucified.

MICHELANGELO'S *PIÈTA DI PALESTRINA*

Unfinished masterpiece the guidebook says.
Manhandled theme no question — the forceless arm
Web-fingered, the head's carriage come to harm,
Impracticable limbs; the Mother's gaze.
A column's capital fronting the last phase
Of the bouleversement, startled this side alarm,
Re-mothering Mother, rock of John's limpet calm:
Is hurriedness the hammerer, hacking praise?

Shortfall — overleap — of art's acme? How is conceived
Creation Prototype crushed but with collapse
Of creatures, world order's rudiments in relapse
To chaos; God's images, God being bereaved,
Lurching towards uncreation — until all is retrieved
As certain fibres about these limbs unclasp?

THE TURIN SHROUD

Bright darkens, black is white; unlit in a tray
Chemicals recycle. The emergence speaks
Spectral revenance, in passion apparel, love-leaks
Laced: Love's extinct star, débâcle, doomsday,
Love with ill's might mismatched the cerements say.
Otherwise the actual: Whose reliquary reeks
Of all abasement, tomorrow overpeaks
All grandeur, gathers universal sway.

Here's not good's Golgotha but palaestra of power.
If God's Son stays with us in this rendition,
Out-delving our deeps, must it not be with mission
That we not unbelieve, unhope or cower
Before worst's worst — seedbed of Paradise flower
Should we at last, alas, grasp faith's transposition?

TU ES SACERDOS

Be simple now and steadfast. You will move
In echoing places, stepping in others' praise,
Measured by memory of precarious days,
Building on laid foundations. You must prove
Your lineage in the ancestry of love
Whose proving is in giving, being a phase
In an employment to make all world ways
Emmaus roads, all journeys end above.

Be steadfast now and footsure who employ
God with a word; be suppliant who must keep
Energies unmanmastered, spoils of no cheap
Huckstering, Godbloodpurchases; who deploy
And hazard vicarious victory, ravage or reap
Hereafter harvests, fulfil Christ or destroy.

SAINT OLIVER PLUNKETT

11 October 1975

After sick silence a voice to invigorate when
Sickness, silence remit; flame on a hill
Flickering above mist and morass until
Caught on a far peak and outsped again
(Space signals so hope-whisper beyond sense's ken);
A dark night's lantern; steppingstone that will
Foothold diaspora instinct to fulfil
Horizon-hid purposes, sore-served: of such men

As outcrop centuries — patriarch, prophet, saint,
Wilderness couriers in God's People's story
Oliver was, trudging by-roads to foothill glory,
Spur to the faltering, crutch to faith fallen faint.
Enskied at the last by grace of the justice junket,
Rally faith-falterers now, Saint Oliver Plunkett!

POOR CLARE CHRISTMAS

Belfast 1974

Their eyes are quiet waters; they move, speak
In interdeference, pressureless, unloud,
Unstirred by urgencies, soul-soldered, a crowd
Only by head-count; for contestation weak
Counter to engines, energies that wreak
A city's ruin might raised, raised too world's proud
Appurtenance might haunts with mushroom cloud:
Against force forceless, whisper combating shriek.

She said, *Our Christmas vigil is for adoring*
Christ in the Sacrament. . . . I saw outpouring
Resources from life's wellspring, power's being;
Levers undamming omnipotence, restoring
To mercy extravagance, need avidity, freeing
Divinity from trammels of our unseeing.

THE POPE IN IRELAND

September 1979

He was larger than eye's seeing as world watched
His Pentecostal emergence from the dark
When each heard each's tongue pronounce his stark
And Petrine summons from lineament notched
By crooked cross and sickle that had scotched
A people's soul; his restiveness the mark
Of spirit enterprise, strength apt to nark
For very forbearance, Mount-sermon theme unblotched.

Storm-weathered priest, be landmark to our land,
Likened to yours, high-hoisted in your favour;
Tutor and guide us, where our bent is other,
The orthodoxies of hate to countermand —
As you in deeper difference — to be neighbour
Across Samaritan fences, brother to brother.

BELFAST CHRISTMAS

1975

In earth's elemental war of death and life
Rampage of winter famine microbe flood
By stages effortfully are stemmed, withstood.
Not so our making's Minotaur, inborn strife:
Forgotten its infancy of sling and knife,
Adult now, adept of atom and lightning, shod
With space-shoes, making earth inert sod
Should men stay savage — doom forebodings rife,

Our part to make killing customary, cheap?
A bar's clientele mangles to charnel heap;
Murder across peace-net volleys; beside Christmas cards
Mails carry instruments of unkind regards;
Death strikes indifferent from vehicle that bombards
At random, from footsteps that to quiet doors creep.

THE NORTHERN QUESTION

Our canyon is in constitutional law:
What ties shall bind to which neighbour; under what name,
Hero or shibboleth or obsolete aim
We march; from which myth-cycle purpose draw.
Records are raked for warranty and flaw
And ashes disinterred for oriflamme,
Charge accosts charge, claim invites counter-claim;
Life's packaging, not life our matter . . . I saw

Two daughters through their mother's Requiem
Cling to a father, tear-spent, astray in grief;
A hospital's overnight rough-reaped harvest sheaf —
Bomb-burgled bodies asway across living's hem —
And knew that bestiality can stem
From the immoderate mind, our enemy-in-chief.

CAUPONANTES BELLUM

Because we have wrapped in rhetoric everything done
Dangerously to serve us with no heed
To reckon service on merits that exceed
Interest, flaunted the ethic of the gun,
We have reneged on faith of father to son,
The good half-story told that must mislead,
Sown what malforms, fertilised pest and weed.
Is it not time being adult was begun

When history plays changing chairs with fable
(Fashioned to be more felt than understood)
And true with false in enterprise to enable
War's travesty, bootleg of murder-clod,
Embezzle patriot patrimony and label
In service of another god than God?

QUO VADIS

We skidded by the edge of two world wars;
We grow in numbers; our allotted earth
Outriches reckoning. Against these set new-birth
Of savage custom which fulfilment bars.
For all-redeeming asset we are heirs
To fifteen centuries of our fathers' faith,
Unbroken if often unlived by, bedrock faith
Wherewith no earth inheritance compares.

We enter the world scene when worldliness
Speaks loudest; shall we, hitherto upholders
Of pristine Europe — once its austere restorers
After collapse — drift into faithlessness
Even now when multiplicities of distress
Arise from easing Christ's yoke from men's shoulders?

September 1983

JESU DULCIS MEMORIA

Jesus of memory, lost to view,
If hearts may burn with thought of you
What thought can morning what must be
The high noon of your company?

No voice no music sense may hear
Quivers like your name in the ear,
No keepsakes bring remoteness near
Like those these syllables endear.

Jesus, whose flesh is food, blood drink,
Once savoured you make viands shrink
To ashes, all who taste conspire
Towards your monopoly of desire.

Jesus, love's goal, foothold of hope,
By whom, towards whom, we limp and grope
How we have reached to you through tears,
From out circumference of fears!

Jesus, swift highway of return
From sin, prompt Yes to all who yearn,
Heaven-host to gibbet-sharing thief,
What plight repulses your relief?

No tongue of prophet shall declare
No deeps of Scripture yield to air
Intimacies your discoverers share,
Joy's consummates beyond time's wear.

The tokens, Jesus, we have of you
On earth, transfigure and imbue
With realness of divinity
Beside you through eternity.

VEXILLA REGIS

Behold the standard of the King,
The emblem of the mystery
Of Life embracing death to bring
Life to the world and victory.

Here hung the body for our cheer
Blooded and watered when a spear
Released the flood whereby the smear
Of our offence is carried clear.

Salute the effigy of death
By David distantly foreknown,
Inaugurating for men's faith
God's reign upon a wooden throne.

O modest and exuberant tree
Seeded of Eden ancestry
And crimson-flashed for royalty,
What high-born limbs have hallowed thee!

O precious scale on which was laid
The recompense the Rescuer paid
When our transgression was outweighed
And Satan's injury unmade.

Hail to the cross, our single trust,
Our trophy of the Passiontide,
Come with fresh blessing to the just,
The sinner and the sin divide.

All praise to you, Blest Trinity,
Salvation's source, God One in Three:
Crown now accredited victory
With spoils spanning eternity.

HORACE TO VIRGIL

Odes, 1, 24

Now is an hour of sorrow unreproved
And spendthrift tears for one two poets loved.
Come, sad Melpomene, bring
Your lyre and bleakly sing.

So our Quintilius sleeps eternally.
When shall such gentleness and modesty
Honour and truth and faith
Again inherit breath?

Quintilius is dead. Who is not grieved?
And you Virgil are first of the bereaved,
You who will plead in vain
With gods ungiving again.

If you plucked strings stronger than Orpheus played
You could not spirit blood to a pale shade —
Come world-about when trees
Pirouette to melodies.

Those whom the god has touched and signed below
Answer assizes no tears overthrow.
Sufferance alone, my friend
Tempers what will not mend.

KITCHEN SEMINAR

The turf fire whirred on and on
Through the bars of its black bastion,
Warmth in the waxen sheen
Of kerosene.
I remember each attitude
Where we sat and stood.

Work Scheme, from house chore she averred,
And Progress Record
I've slipped up on: You rein nimble word.

I remember the coal-glossy look
Of the entry book
Where children are c,h,n,
And sequence is sovereign;
And — so genes repercuss, interhook —
The sombre green book
His son of four years,
All eyes and ears,
He was showing, where appears
An angel-face Shelley, a fire on
Whose drownedness had haloed one Byron.

I forgot to ask why
Such matter to mystify
One so much one's son.
Did it fall out casually?
Or from feeling a child must be told
Life ends, and not just for the old;
A child whose father might die
Tomorrow out of the sky?

AFTER CHESTERTON

That God can make a tree
Even a child can see;
With God for agency
All's made that can be thought.
What takes the breath away
Is hearing say
A tree climbs to obey
Dictates of mindless clay.
What faith unfaith has brought!

SLEEP AND THE MUSES

We must not slight the Muses though they keep
Coming with second thoughts through half the night.
In gleanings harvested by after-light
Others may find the recipe for sleep.

WHIT SUNDAY

The earth is garlanded to acclaim the power
That fuels its renovations. Ours to ensway
Sun of the soul within our hearts today,
Greenfingering seedlings of grace's flower.

NIGHT PRAYER

The day's imperatives answer night's recall
And night's arrest our gadgetry enfolds.
Mother and child the same oblivion holds.
Be you our vigilance now, Master of all.

ÁR nATHAIR

Meabhraidh a Chríost, gí géar ár scoilt,
Gur aon is Athair dúinn is Duit.

PREACHER'S PRAYER

Lord, send me thinking wise and true,
Compact and redolent of You;
And have the Fire-tongued score me speech
Tuned to the mystery I preach.

Bring then my listeners to receive
What's said, and actuate and achieve.
And last, the wisdom I relay
Might it have spillage on the way?

A VOICE AGAINST JUSTICE

(from the Irish)

It is not justice I pursue,
That's the last thing I want of you:
Too well I know the score that's due:
Look, Christ, what I have done undo.

HOC PASSIONIS TEMPORE

(from the Greek)

From passion and Holy Rood,
Covenanting Blood
In cleansing Flood
Flow in me unwithstood.

PRESENT TENSE

I am the present, I'm a fork of hay
Skied to tomorrow out of yesterday
I am the actual, freedom's girth of play.
Yesterday and tomorrow
are hollow.

SPRING

A shoot
Has taken root,
First buds unfold;
Fever to see
The accomplished tree
Shivers at being old.

BELFAST

Belfast is walled by mountain and moated by sea
And undermined by deposits of history.

SPRING IN A SEED SHOP

'My lawn is running wild, I need' —
From one — 'what extirpates the weed'.
'The Spring's a marvel' — for counter-neighbour —
'Give me what granaries my bees' labour'.

ON THE ANTRIM COAST ROAD

Here one may recognise
The aptness of twin eyes,
Deferring respectively
To caper of land and sea.

CRIONA

Eventually freed
Of the kill-by-kindness weed
Criona contrived to win
His tug-of-war with gin.

The hazards of infection
Preempted by injection,
When the word was Eat no Fat
For Criona that was that.

A car's length Criona hasn't
Driven without seatbelt fastened.
He never walked by night
Without something white.

Criona insured against
Invoiced ill intent
But unforesaw a bus
Flush with a moment's fuss.

A SHROPSHIRE LAD

You own God's handiwork in a May shower —
With faith of pouting fist —
But when a cherry tree becomes a flower
Are you an atheist?

GRACE AFTER TV COSMOLOGY

The wider our probings uncover
Infinities of order and plan
The louder we toast one another
Pouring libations to man

BISEACH NA GAOITHE

Níl gaoth dá séideann
Gan rath d'áit eígín.

COLD OBSTRUCTION. . .

(*From the Irish*)

Earth grovels where I choose to tread
But there are different days ahead
When a whistle blows for change-place play
With me subservient to clay.

AGE OF DISCRETION

(*From the Welsh*)

No man past forty, let him laugh like a leafy tree,
Hears a vault door creak without flashing a little less glee.

FELL SERGEANT

(*From the Welsh*)

Death isn't one to serve notice: His reminders are pain, loss of pep
There's no taking note of his features, no memorising his step.

ON REMEMBERING NEIL KEVIN

We grieve and trade his jests till grief is mended
And grieve again because his jests are ended.

WHERE GODS AGREE

Surely death is disaster: how otherwise should
Dying have been abjured by every god?

Sappho

AN APPLE. . .

. . . An apple blushes topmost on a tree,
A tall tree's crest fruit-pickers failed to see —
Or saw, so far it was, it must be free. . . .

Sappho

A HYACINTH. . .

. . . A hyacinth, lightening a mountain pass,
Trampled by shepherds is bedded now in grass. . . .

Sappho

BY THE MERIDIAN OF KEEM

I have been through Connemara, the fine scenery of which is less known than it should be. Furbough House stands amidst beautiful woods, an Eden in a wilderness of rocks and treeless waste. The whole neighbourhood is most singular.

Gerard Manley Hopkins
(*in a letter to Robert Bridges, 1884*)

From Erris Head to Cashla Bay
Many's the road that runs astray
But miles and hours are in light esteem
By the Meridian of Keem,
Which is no mark for an intense
And bigoted cult of commonsense.

Consider how we provide to know
If we have got where we aim to go.
Maamturk, Maam Cross, Maamtrasna, Maam —
Isn't the point about a name
Half lost if it keeps half the same?
Lettermore, Letter, Lettermullen,
Moyard, Moyode, Moycullen —
How far are -ard -ode -ullen the better
Of commonage like Moy and Letter?
Whatever we're short on we've words galore;
Must Tullys and Invers litter the shore?

When you've got the length of Tubbernaveen
Ireland has quit wearing the green
And church and schoolhouse will be found
By Killary and Achill Sound
Without homestead eye-lengths around.

Cattle have wished their horns on sheep
And both are black and nibble steep
Insalubrious mountaintop
Sooner than walled field's pallid crop.
But fields are few and bogs are many
Where Murrisk tidals lap Mulranny
And under Cruachan and Slievemore
What goes for bog is thin and poor.

The coastline south of Letterfrack
Is so eaten into and beaten back,
So messed with adjacent islands, wet spaces
And seawrack braving apartheid places
There's trouble knowing which way one faces.
Inlets and rivers roll north, reel south
In capers: be said by word of mouth.

From Renvyle Point to Barna strand
There's not a straight line on the land.
Earth's crust is toothed and scarred and twisted
Hillocks are humped and many-fisted
And man's inveiglings are resisted.

Nothing is smooth soft level fine
To windward of the Curragh Line —
Unless when, remiss or of faltering purpose,
Winds may let up on a lake surface.
Stone-crochet walls enmesh encurtain
And lurch to lean on granite boulders
And leap to lanyard murderous shoulders
And unbiased tree is as strangely seen
As a stone's throw of unstony green
Times you could be unsettled here
About the season of the year.

Who breaks the cipher, reads the heart
Of a topsyturvydom apart?
What primal chaos has it outlasted?
By what catacylsm was it blasted?
Were the embroideries all gone
When the Couturier reached the Conn?
(For the endearments of Pontoon
Owe little to silver spoon
And poets totting Mayo's abundance
Are they not accountants of love's redundance?)
Or was bracken adequate for Connacht —
Let whoever try upholstery on it?

Perish absurd imaginings,
Ironical disparagings!
Here is full wardrobe and to spare
Of idiosyncratic wear
Less platitude of curve and square.
No precipitate this of cosmic antic
But Consort of unwooed Atlantic,
Breakwater, barrier, boundary-fence,
Outwork of two continents.
This half-the-world's end harbours only
Anti-beauty, lunar-lonely,
Grandeur inordinate and strange,
Got of tempest on mountain range.

Whoever is at odds with city
Or country coerced to being pretty,
Who jibs at all that's grooved and set
And morselled out by timepiece hand,
Who carries that he must forget
Will disencumber and lightly stand
Freeman of aboriginal land

Unsubjugate since its peaks were shaped
And — not for year-round costume — draped
In brown and gold and red and green,
Arched-over blue, diaphanous-clean —
Primals and inchoates between
In quivering commerce, uncatalogued nameless
Resolving dissolving where all is changeless.

Who has tracked elemental anger,
Or brushed with archetypes of danger,
Till he has watched earth air and ocean
In seismic tantrum and commotion
Contesting how certain rocks align
That string Broadhaven Stags with Slyne?
And who has summed the Summer's gift
Not having seen, as cloud-cocoons lift,
The alchemies that sunlight bakes
On furtive Connemara lakes,
Doolough Inagh Kylemore
Nafooey Finnlough and sundry more
In posture of moats outflung before
Keeps of uncommerceable ore?

Here gentleness wrestles with rude
And there is housing for each mood
And spirit's super-substantial food.
Here are mountain-populous places
Mountains in multiple embraces,
The wind their word across birdless spaces;
Mountains to ambuscade, imprison
Or viaduct to larger vision,
Mountains with sphinxes granite-hewn
In ward of deserts, tombstone-strewn;

Skyline of calligraphy's first paces
Or screenings of lost cardiac races;
Lakes that cling to roads that meander,
Lakes in gaggle of geese and gander
In malformation *untereinander*;
Furrowed ocean astir without pause
Now in war-dance of whitening claws
Now contrite and docile to benign laws.

Here is call for mirth and wonder
Until Earth girders creak and sunder,
For early entry and late delaying,
Coming to mock, for prayer staying:
Habilamented to deprive,
More richly giving than soils that thrive,
Wilderness near as may be alive.

Here are Earth oracles to advise —
Or one who taught by bush and cloud,
Who silent, stones would cry aloud,
Whose wisdom comes contrariwise —
Of riches of mind and heart and eyes
And beauty tricked out in disguise;
Of wasteland pleading, Leave us unknown;
Of living not by bread alone
(Be not solicitous lay not up,
There's many a slip between lip and cup);
Of ethic of toiling not nor spinning
(So much is lost for a worthless winning)
How what unglitters belittles gold;
How no story's issue is ever all told,
And when the arithmetic is done
How slender the margins under the sun.

Throne-sharer with Father and Spirit, Source and Son
Only-begotten of the Unorigined One
Through Whom is made all that is meant to be,
Spare for the maker of this book, for me,
Until the hurdled loop of life is run
The care that keeps one of your company.

From the Greek Anthology